MY JOURNEY TO FINDING MY

IDENTITY, CALLING & ASSIGNMENT

And the difference in the three!

BY

SUSAN COOPER CREEL

My Journey to Finding My Identity, Calling & Assignment – And the Difference in the Three

Paperback ISBN: 978-1-953806-48-2
EBook ISBN: 978-1-953806-49-9
Library of Congress: 2021913446

Editor: Robin McEachen
Publisher: Spotlight Publishing™ - https://SpotlightPublishing.Pro
Cover Design: Angie Anayla with AdobeStock photos
Interior Design: Amit Dey

Website: www.SusanCreel.com

MY JOURNEY TO FINDING MY IDENTITY, CALLING & ASSIGNMENT

And the difference in the three!

BY

SUSAN COOPER CREEL

Goodyear, AZ

Reviews

"Plagued with questions of what is my calling and purpose and does my VERY secular and demanding career align with Jesus plans for my life, Susan's book met me in my own season of an identity crisis. Susan's transparent journey helped me see that I am on an assignment that does NOT negate my identity or my calling."

~ LeeAnn K.
Age 40, Wife, Mother,
Chemical Sales, and a heart for Jesus.

"Interesting, thought-provoking read that takes you past yesterday and beyond tomorrow. This book will be on my gift-giving list for ALL of my daughters AND my granddaughters!"

~ LaVon M.
Age 69, Wife, Mother,
Grandmother, and avid reader.

"A roadmap to guide you through every stage and phase of life!"

~Robin M.
Age 39, Masters in Education, wife, mother,
bereaved mother, educator.

"I am a widow, a mom and a grandmother on the large scale of my life but in moments of my life I have been a student, a business owner, and an employee. This book confirmed what assignments are life long and which are just for a moment or season of my life."

~ Casey W.
Age 48, Widow, Mom, Grandmother

Table of Contents

Dedicated To

MY AMAZING RED-HEADED DAUGHTER

KATE LYNN CREEL

MAY YOU NEVER HAVE TO WALK THE SAME ROAD

WITHOUT REALIZING THAT THERE ARE THOSE WHO HAVE GONE BEFORE YOU

♡Mom

TO MY MOM AND DAD

ROYCE AND JENNIFER COOPER

FOR PUSHING ME TO DO THIS

IN A KIND YET EMPHATIC WAY

♡Susan

TO MY HUSBAND

DARREN CREEL

FOR ALWAYS LOVING ME

AND ALWAYS PAYING

♡Beautiful

Foreword

Few things in life speak louder than simply being consistent. You are who you are but not everyone always knows it… not so with Susan Creel. For more than 30 years, I have watched Susan grow from a young college girl to a wife, mother, businesswoman, missionary, teacher, author and valued friend. Those who know her… know her. Her life is an open book which serves to encourage everyone she meets.

Susan and her husband Darren started life together with nothing more than their love for each other, and their faith in God. Life didn't always seem to cooperate, but nonetheless, they managed. Susan's contribution to this winning team was the perfect ingredient, added at just the right time to hold them steady and push them forward to success. They now own multiple businesses in southeast Texas and support several spiritually motivated humanitarian relief efforts worldwide. True servants, they never stop growing, giving, and going.

One of the things I dearly love about Susan is her enthusiastic approach to the next step in God's plan for her life. I've never known her to shrink back from any challenge, no matter how arduous it may seem. She's a woman of prayer who is committed to the Word of God with a heart to participate in the Great Commission. Those who attend the groups she leads, whether business or church related, leave with valuable nuggets that soon become principles on which they too can build a successful life, marriage, and family.

Her story of finding God's best path for her life will draw the reader along to understand that the journey is your friend. It is the journey that prepares us to operate at destiny's capacity. Prepare yourself to be challenged and inspired. Your greatest day is yet ahead.

R. L. Hammonds,
Sr. Pastor of Golden Triangle Church on the Rock

Introduction

The Word of God is like glitter...if you open it, it gets all over you.

I did not set out to write a book.

When I started this journey, it felt like the most excruciating thing I had ever been through. I was frustrated, tired, angry, and my self-esteem was the lowest it had ever been. Almost immediately, I knew I could not walk through this without Jesus Christ (I say almost because my red-headed stubbornness was convinced I could fix my current situation, but I was wrong.)

What you will be reading in these next pages started as a letter to my daughter, Kate. She was in her late teens when this journey began for me, and I knew she was watching. Despite my God-given anti-fragility mindset, I was not able to barrel through this like I had other challenges in my life. But I was trying to raise an adult, and I knew I needed to show her how to walk this path if she ever found herself on the same one.

As I came out of the deepest parts of this journey, I decided to write her an exceptionally long letter detailing my voyage through the depression and the loss of self I had experienced. It was meant to be my hearts prayer written for her in case she ever had to walk this trek as well. I wanted her to know that others had walked it before and there was no reason to reinvent this wheel.

As I wrote, I was able to organize my story in a way that I was able to repeat it to others. Before I knew it, the story was flowing out of me and into the lives of others. (There is something about writing things down that helps you process it). Soon after I finished, I was asked to speak at a small women's Bible study. I knew exactly what God wanted me to share. The women at the meeting (Holla to my Apache Sisters!) were very receptive to my story, incredibly supportive of its message and several identified with the journey I had traveled.

One of those ladies asked me for my notes to share with a young women's group she led. That night, I did not have notes. I had spoken extemporaneously from my heart, so I tried to email her a copy of the letter I had written to Kate. It would not email due to its size, so I posted it on Facebook for her to download. But then I forgot about it for several hours. By the time I remembered, there were several comments from people who were blessed by it. Months later, I received a mandate from my father, Royce Cooper that this needed to be a book.

HOW TO STUDY THE WORD

The first thing I realized at the beginning of this trial was that even though I had been reading my Bible for years, I had never learned to STUDY it. My daily Bible reading was more of a checklist item (and I am sad to say it was left unchecked on most days).

Now, we have a saying in our Bible 101 Study that "The Word of God is like glitter. If you open it, it will get all over you!." It is true. If you are like I was and are just reading your Bible, it is still working on you. The Word of God will NOT return void. But this battle was going to require a deeper dive into God's Word. I needed it IN me, not just ON me…and I did not know how to start.

I found a Bible study method called SOAP and is a method I still use today. I did not invent this method and have had no luck in finding who was the original creator of the method, but God bless them for sharing it!

SOAP is an acronym that stands for:

S – Scripture

O – Observations

A – Application

P – Prayer

Here is how to start:

- Grab a Journal, spiral notebook or whatever you can find and your Bible (or an online version like www.biblegateway.com).
- Then choose a book, a story, or a person in the Bible like Ruth, John, or Esther
  - I highly recommend studying the book of Ruth. The story of an amazing woman who was in a tough situation but by following her calling, became the great, great, great (+31!) grand-mother of Jesus. Her willingness to be faithful, available, and teachable even when others believed she had no future, positioned her to be in the direct lineage of Jesus Christ. Wow!
  - In the first workbook portion of this book, we will be using this method to study our identity.
- Then just follow the acronym in your journal:
  - S – Scripture: WRITE the verse in your own handwriting.

    - ❑ As I said before, and your English teacher before me, when you WRITE something with your hands it sinks in a little deeper. Your muscles literally ingest the information you are writing. Experts have shown that handwriting something helps you to remember it better! It also improves your memory of the subject and increases your focus on it.
    - ❑ Do not skip this step if possible. It is vitally important.
- ❍ O – Observation: What about this scripture jumped out at you? A city, A person? An event or a cultural note? Perhaps something you are not even sure what it means! Write those down then do some research.
- ❍ A – Application: Now, how can you apply this scripture and what you have learned to your life? Do you have some beliefs that need to change? Some stinkin' thinkin' that needs to be stopped? Maybe there is something you need to START doing? Write those down.
- ❍ P – Prayer: Now write and SAY a prayer to God about how you would like to change. Just talk to Him like you would talk to a friend. Thank Him for what He has done for you. Perhaps you need to ask forgiveness for something he has shown you that you have been doing that is against His will for your life.

I am convinced that if you are new to studying your Bible, that this method will give you an outline to start. It will create a successful habit in your day to day reading of the Word and that habit will become a craving that will draw you back to the Word of God daily. That craving will call to you when you miss your quiet time and in times of need the words that you have studied will be a comfort and a resource for you to encourage yourself and others.

I am sure of it. It has happened to me and many others.

We teach this method in our Bible 101 study as we are going through each book of the Bible. The more you study the Word, the more if will reveal its strength to you. One day, you will be walking through a storm in life and the Word of God will be the first thing you think of! You will encourage yourself with scriptures, bolster a friend who is needing some strength like yours and pray these scriptures back to God as you remind Him of His promises. His is a Living Word. Each time you read it you will get something new. He promises it will happen.

I have included some examples of SOAPing in the Appendix of this book. Check those out before you keep reading!

HOW TO READ THIS BOOK

You could read this entire book in one short sitting, but it took me four and a half years to walk. This roadmap (a sort of bread crumb trail for you and my daughter) should take time for you to navigate. It will be tempting to read the entire book and skip the workbook pages. I beg you not to do that. Blazing through these pages will certainly do something rather than nothing for you, but the real treasure is the habits, deeper relationship with Jesus Christ and personal epiphanies that will happen when you take your time. I challenge you to take this slowly.

As I expanded the original letter into the format you see here, I continued to picture several nameless and faceless women in my Spirit. Consistently in my prayer time, I saw two pictures. A group of young women, new Christians, maybe who have struggled in their past and are now looking toward a greater future with Christ but unsure of a specific path how to get there. The other, a woman going through a transition in her life and feeling hemmed in, unsure if she is in the right spot or what she should be doing, a little tired or a lot tired. Whether you are one of those women or any woman in between, there is something here for you, but it happens in a day-to-day relationship with Christ.

I realize that many of you will want to spend a lot of time in each section. That is okay.

That is what I hope for. It's even okay to read the first section, work a few pages of homework and then put it down for several days to mediate on what you've been soaking in then pick it back up when you're ready. I'm okay with that too.

In fact, that is exactly how I walked this journey. One teeny tiny step at a time.

By the time you reach the assignment portion of this book, my prayer is that you have worked the homework to completion. In doing so, and praying as you go, your heart will be deeply plowed and tuned in to the voice of God to hear your current assignment. I know He will do it and I am praying for you as you navigate this roadmap.

Your steps have been ordered by God. He knew you would have this book in front of you at this moment. While you were making your biggest mistake, living a boring life, or fulfilling a great challenge, He was orchestrating the symphony of your life to come to this point. And guess what, He is still creating the masterpiece called you.

I pray this book leads you deeper into
His Word, His Will, and his desires for you.

Chapter 1

Fired by God

I loved my job. It made me feel accomplished and gave me a purpose.

Creel Investments was in its 21st year. Darren, my husband, and I had been working with God's grace to lead and to build our property management company and now employed 25+ team members, managed over a thousand units in our four-county region and worked for 350+ clients from all over the nation and some from around the world.

Personally, we had a beautiful daughter who was graduating from high school and headed to a local college to pursue a degree in graphic design. Our marriage was stronger than ever. We still enjoyed working together, still enjoyed dinner together, and still enjoyed each other's company. We were all good.

My role at Creel Investments was Vice-President in charge of Sales and Acquisitions. I signed new clientele, pitched our services, helped investors buy and sell properties in their portfolios. Then, I would then hand their investments off to the management and maintenance teams for the daily administration. It was a role that I thrived in doing because it was a mix of sales and networking, two things I excelled at and enjoyed. Darren, who is not a salesperson or social type per say, recognized that I was valuable in this arena and so, while he managed the decisions on the business side of things, I was perfectly happy on the 'adding business' side of things.

Beginning in the fall of 2017, the Lord began to speak to me about moving out of my position. Ever so gently and in subtle ways, I begin to hear a soft voice nudging me to make a change. I consistently pushed the notion aside telling myself that Darren needed me, that I was making a difference and that this was my role in our business, marriage, and life.

I was wrong.

I was wrong to ignore it. I was wrong to elevate myself above the plans of God in my life.

I was wrong all the way around.

In May of 2018 on a random Wednesday, I woke up to the voice of God almost screaming in my ears. It was not audible (it was so much louder than that). But it clearly got my attention. What He said was "*You HAVE to get out so that HE can!*"

I immediately knew that I was holding up the plans Darren had made to hand the controlling reigns of the company over to our property manager and eventually sell the company to her. If I were working in the company, Darren would feel an obligation to stay and work alongside me. I had to get out of the company so that he could get out of the company eventually.

Now the mandate to remove myself from my role was impossible to ignore and I realized that I had disobeyed the urging of the Holy Spirit for too long. Now my obedience was critical, and I knew what needed to happen.

Early that morning while still lying in bed, I prayed for forgiveness. When Darren and I sat down for breakfast, I told him all that God had been telling me for the past several months and the mandate that He had given me. Darren's response was so unexpected. He lowered his head and quietly said, "Oh thank goodness, I wasn't shore how to tell you." God himself, just fired me.

Darren had been feeling like he wanted me to step back but he knew it would devastate me and leave me feeling unnecessary and unimportant. He did not want to be the one that told me so he prayed that God would do it. But then his stubborn red-headed wife would not listen. When I finally relented, he was relieved. And I'm sure God was as well.

I had been fired from the company before. Once to go home and be with our daughter Kate who was born prematurely and again while walking through IKEA. Darren had decided he had wanted me to step back from the company in Kate's middle school years. Her dyslexia had made every grade something she had to fight for, and she needed my full-time support. But I had convinced myself that the company was smaller then and my role was less "important."

I went to work that morning and immediately began to train my incredibly capable assistant to duplicate me and removed myself from the office day to day happenings. In two weeks, I was jobless.

The first two weeks after I left, I kept busy by obsessively organizing my house, deep cleaning every nook and cranny, and cleaning out closets for donations. Nothing was safe. I tried to tell myself that after a few weeks without me, God would see my worth in my former position and let me go back to work. But God was clear that I was no longer supposed to be there. I was jobless, but with a really clean house.

September 1st, I began to get ready for deer season at Gibson's Deer Processing, one of our other companies in Port Neches, Texas. I ordered supplies, deep cleaned the shop, reworked the advertising. It was just another way to stay busy. Another way to stay "important." Soon after, on October 1st, deer season started. For the next 3-4 months, we were up to our elbows in deer meat, so I pushed down the depressing 'you-don't-have-a-job-after-this' feeling hoping that something would change before the end of deer season.

But then, it happened. Deer season ended, and I slowly slipped into a depression. I never thought I could feel so unimportant or unnecessary. I prayed for direction, argued with God, scoured my Bible for answers, and cried my eyes out daily. I could not find a reason to get out of bed in the mornings and drifted into misery that I couldn't pull myself out of. No matter how many lunches I had with friends, projects I started and finished or budget busting shopping sprees I enjoyed, I still felt discarded and worthless. To be honest, most people in my life had no idea I was struggling so deeply. I had grown up in church and was an expert at hiding my true feelings and battles. I could put on a happy face while at church or lunch, but when I retreated to my car or home, I dropped the façade immediately.

Friends were so kind to listen and encourage me, but even while being uplifted I felt embarrassed. Not because I was being needy or sad, but because I felt unusable, demoted, and unimportant. Some of my closest friends (you know who you are!), were quite honest with me and argued my worth outside of the corporate world. One dear friend reminded me that the volunteer work I was doing with a local women's ministry was making a dramatic difference. But I could not see it. Her pep talks always helped but it was always a temporary relief. I would soon slip back into the same lonely place.

I continued to argue with God that "I have more in me than this!" I could DO more, I wanted to do more. I wanted to BE more.

He would gently remind me through friends, songs, sermons, and even podcast that He knew the plans he had for me and that they were good plans (Jeremiah 29:11). But all I could feel was the pain. All I could see was the loss.

I do not remember the day that I finally hit rock bottom. I just remember a dark time in my life when the anger, loneliness and depression controlled my thoughts and emotions until I finally cried out to the Lord to help me.

When the Apostle Peter stepped out of a small fishing boat in the middle of a raging storm to walk on water to Jesus (Matthew 14:29) He took his eyes off the Lord and began to focus on the storm. It was then, when he focused on the troubles around him, that he began to sink into the water. But Jesus was there. Jesus reached out and grabbed him in the moment of his greatest need. And just like He was with Peter, He was right there for me, waiting to grab me. Waiting for me to REALLY put my eyes on Him. I spent the next month's grappling with concepts of who I was, why I was here, and what I was supposed to be doing. This wrestling is where I found the "Identity, Calling and Assignment" ideas. With the help of ONE chapter in ONE book (*H3 Leadership – Be Hungry, Stay Humble, Always Hustle by Brad Lomenick*) I found my next job. I needed to find the answers to those three things.

And so, it began...

Chapter 2

Questioning My Identity

In the United States when we meet someone new, one of the first questions we often ask is "What do you do?" It has become a way to learn more about that person, a sneak peek into who they are. If the answer impresses us, we consider that person to be someone we should know. If it does not...we may not even remember their names and may even jump to a judgement of who we think they "really" are.

We have successfully placed our roles in life in the position of identity. Our jobs, our spouses, our kids, our chapter in life (motherhood/fatherhood) our family name or even our wounds can become a measure of who we are and our value. We judge others and ourselves by job/life descriptions. We believe that our role must be one of some importance to be worthy of our respect. Only then can we be called "successful."

This dichotomy was perfectly exemplified at the beginning of the Covid-19 global pandemic when overnight the phrase "essential worker" dominated our evening news. Suddenly NFL football players and Grammy award winning pop musicians were stuck at home while supermarket cashiers were deemed essential and worked on the frontlines keeping this country fed.

I have heard stay at home moms (one of the MOST important jobs ever) answer the question "What do you do?" with 'domestic engineer, household CEO and director of child development.' Creative, No doubt. But why do they feel the need to elevate the obvious answer to sound important? Because our society thinks that the role of a stay-at-home mom is less important and not as glamorous as 'Domestic engineer.' If we are not careful, society, social media and our own stinkin' thinkin' will warp our sense of identity.

As I walked through this journey, I realized almost immediately that I had to change my answer to the question. For years, I would proudly answer with a bold "Vice-president of Creel Investments Inc." but now I was jobless, and I didn't know how to answer the questions of 'what did I do.'

I began by asking myself a series of questions.

Who are you?

Who do you want to be?

How do you describe yourself?

What is your profile description on Facebook?

My answers to these questions almost always ended up sounding like I was applying for a job.

- "I am a wife, a mom, a business owner."
- "I want to help people all over the world change their world."
- "I am a goal oriented, self-motivated person."

My Facebook biography literally said, "Vice President, Creel Investments Inc, Realtor."

And although all those things are true. They are NOT my identity. At least they should not have been. I had NO IDEA where to begin to find my true identity.

During all of this, I heard a song called "Who I Am" by Jessica Andrews, and it became my theme song for this moment.

> *"I am Rose Marie's granddaughter, the spitting image of my father, and when the day is done my momma's still my biggest fan. Sometimes, I'm clueless and I'm clumsy, but I got friends that love me, and they know just where I stand. It's all a part of me. And that's who I am."*

I would put it on repeat and blare the music while I sang it at the top of my lungs almost as a war cry. I even changed the lyrics to declare that I was Lillian's granddaughter! And that worked for a little while.

It is true. Your mother and father are part of who you are because you carry their DNA. They created you, but the truest part of your identity is the Heavenly Father that knew you 'before I (He) formed you in your mother's womb' (Jeremiah 1:5). Your heavenly father. The Lord God.

This realization prompted a deep dive into who God says that I am. Scripture by scripture I began to study what my heavenly Father said about me, He has a lot to say.

Ephesians 2:10 is just one of the scriptures that I memorized to repeat to myself. It says:

"For we are (I am) his workmanship (masterpiece, creation, handiwork, that which has been made for a work), created in Christ Jesus for good works which God has prepared ahead of time so that we should walk in them."

This scripture is the summary of our identity in Christ. Read it again.

- You are a masterpiece.
- Created to do something good
- Something that GOD himself has prepared for you
- So, you CAN do it!

In the art world, critics decide what defines a work as a masterpiece and we tell ourselves that 'beauty is in the eye of the beholder.' But that is not what the Word declares.

In God's eyes, only the creator of a masterpiece can say what His creation is truly designed to do, say, or mean. I was born in the master's heart, and He is my only creator. I belong to Him, and my worth is only defined BY Him. For too long, I had allowed the world to define my identity and convince me that I am not enough, or ironically, that I was ALL THAT. But God calls me His masterpiece; therefore, I am His and my identity is in Him and Him alone.

The struggle is to not forget that.

In these next several workbook pages you will study and SOAP the Word of God to learn what He says about you. As you begin, I pray that these words will begin to convince you of what God, your heavenly Father, already knows. That you are chosen, called to do a specific work for him, priceless and an important piece to His plan. You may begin to see areas of your life that may need to be tweaked a bit, habits or thought processes that need to be changed. I challenge you. Allow the Word of God to change you. You will never regret it.

~Homework~

"But you are a chosen people, a royal priesthood, a holy nation, God's special possession, that you may declare the praises of him who called you out of darkness into his wonderful light."

1 Peter 2:9

1) Write this scripture in your own handwriting:

2) What does it mean to be chosen? A royal priest?

3) What does this scripture call us to do as His chosen people? His royal family? What did He do for you because you are chosen?

4) Write out a prayer asking God to help you apply this verse to your life and change your image of yourself through His eyes.

~Homework~

"For you are a people holy to the Lord your God. Out of all the peoples on the face of the earth, the Lord has chosen you to be his treasured possession."

Deuteronomy 14:2

1) Write this scripture in your own handwriting:

2) What does it mean to be a "treasured possession"? Do you have a treasure possession? What would you do to protect it, care for it?

3) Do you have a treasured possession? Something that is very precious to you? What would you do to protect it, care for it? Have you forgotten that you are just as special?

4) Write out a prayer asking God to help you apply this verse to your life and change your image of yourself through His eyes.

~Homework~

"For we are God's handiwork, created in Christ Jesus to do good works, which God prepared in advance for us to do."

Ephesians 2:10

1) Write this scripture in your own handwriting:

2) What does it mean to be God's handiwork? What does he ask us to do in this scripture?

3) If you were convinced that you were made by God and He asked you to do something, would you do it? Why or why not?

4) Write out a prayer asking God to help you apply this verse to your life and change your image of yourself through His eyes.

~Homework~

"Now you are the body of Christ, and individual members of it."

1 Corinthians 12:27 (HCS)

1) Write this scripture in your own handwriting:

2) What does it mean to be the body of Christ? Is each part of a body important? Is one part of the body more important than the other?

3) How is my view of myself different than that of God's view of me?
What stinkin' thinkin' do I need to change in my life.

4) Write out a prayer asking God to help you apply this verse to your life and change your image of yourself through His eyes.

~Homework~

"If we confess our sins, He is faithful and righteous to forgive us our sins and to cleanse us from all unrighteousness."

1 John 1:9 (HCS)

1) Write this scripture in your own handwriting:

2) What does it mean to confess our sins? What does it say that HE will do if we confess our sins?

3) Do you have unrighteousness in your life? Have you confessed those sins to God?

4) If not, say this prayer aloud to God right now!

Dear Heavenly Father, please forgive me for the things I've done wrong. I place my faith in Jesus, who died for my sins and made a way for me to have eternal life. Amen.

Now that you have confessed, He has promised He will forgive us and cleanse us.

You are now a child of God.

~Homework~

"See what great love the Father has lavished on us, that we should be called children of God! And that is what we are!"

1 John 3:1a (NIV)

1) Write this scripture in your own handwriting:

2) What does this scripture say that you are? What has He lavished on you?

3) Whose child are you? Have you forgotten? Where do you need to change your thinking?

4) Write out a prayer asking God to help you apply this verse to your life and change your image of yourself through His eyes.

~Homework~

"The Lord your God is with you, the Mighty Warrior who saves.
He will take great delight in you; in his love he will no longer rebuke you,
but will rejoice over you with singing."

Zephaniah 3:17 (NIV)

1) Write this scripture in your own handwriting:

2) Who is the Mighty Warrior? What does it mean to delight in you?

3) What does this scripture say God wants to do for you?

4) Write out a prayer asking God to help you apply this verse to your life and change your image of yourself through His eyes.

~Homework~

"Make your own attitude that of Christ Jesus."

Philippians 2:5 (NIV)

1) Write this scripture in your own handwriting:

2) What is the attitude of Christ Jesus?

3) Who does this scripture say should change attitudes? You or God?
What thoughts, beliefs or attitude do you need to change?

4) Write out a prayer asking God to help you apply this verse to your life and change your image of yourself through His eyes.

~Homework~

I will praise You because I have been remarkably and wonderfully made.
Your works are wonderful, and I know this very well.

Psalms 139:4 (HCS)

1) Write this scripture in your own handwriting:

2) What does it mean to be remarkable and wonderfully made?

3) Why are we supposed to praise Him? Does God make things that are anything less than wonderful? Where do you need to change your thinking?

4) Write out a prayer asking God to help you apply this verse to your life and change your image of yourself through His eyes.

~Homework~

"He Himself bore our sins in His body on the tree, so that, having died to sins, we might live for righteousness; you have been healed by His wounds."

1 Peter 2:24 (HCS)

1) Write this scripture in your own handwriting:

2) What did God do for you on the cross?

3) What wounds do you have that need to be healed by God?

4) Write out a prayer asking God to help you apply this verse to your life and change your image of yourself through His eyes.

~Homework~

"For the Spirit God gave us does not make us timid,
but gives us power, love and self-discipline."

2 Timothy 1:7(HCS)

1) Write this scripture in your own handwriting:

2) What three things does God give us through his Spirit?

3) In what areas of your life have you been timid, weak, and undisciplined?

4) Write out a prayer asking God to help you apply this verse to your life and change your image of yourself through His eyes.

Chapter 3

Finding my Calling

Now that you have studied the scriptures about what God says about you, you may have found yourself thinking to yourself as I did, "but He wrote these words to everyone. It's not specific to just me."

And that is absolutely true. But that is why He CALLS you.

A calling is simply this:

An invitation to be prepared to do something.

Once you have come to accept that you have been called, then you must find what you have been prepared to do.

Romans 11:29 says that *"God's gifts and his call are irrevocable."* Meaning that they are not able to be changed or reversed. They are final. So, no matter what you have done, what bad decisions you have made, or how badly you have messed up your life. You STILL have a call on your life to do something that God has designed only you to do.

Does that mean that you will be the ONLY one doing that calling? Probably not.

You may be called to be a teacher, and though there are not enough good teachers out there, you may be called to be a teacher for a specific little boy or girl. Or perhaps you are a teacher of marriages, pastors, employees, or coworkers. Perhaps you are called to teach your daughter how to be a godly wife or your son how to be a man that follows after God's heart. Teaching is a calling. But it does not have to happen in a classroom.

There is a difference between a calling and a job.

Once you identify your calling you may realize that it may look a lot like a job and can easily be confused with a job. A person can be called to teach, and the obvious assumption would be to get a teaching degree in order to teach in a classroom at your local school district. But as we have already established, teaching can happen in a variety of places.

By the time I got to the point where I was ready to try and find my calling, I was anxious. I had been so confused for so long that I had not even realized how vexed I was. Now that I knew my TRUE identity, I was ready to do what God wanted me to do.

I soon realized that I had no clue about how to find my calling. I had no idea where to start. And by the way, googling 'what is my calling?" is NOT the answer. (Seriously. Don't do it.)

The internet led my down paths like, 'What did you want to be when you were a child?,' 'Roam a library' and my personal favorite, 'Shop around.' I did all kinds of personality test to try and find my purpose in life that mostly ended in statements like "You should be a real estate agent." No kidding. I already AM a real estate agent! And I can tell you. It's a wonderful job and I enjoy it, but if that is my CALLING take me to Heaven now!

Please don't get me wrong. Personality test are great for discovering opportunities and areas of your character that can be honed, but I just knew there was more to it than that.

Feeling a little defeated, I went back to the drawing board.

First, I went to the definition of 'a calling.'

Merriam-Webster defines a "calling" as: *"…a strong inner impulse toward a particular course of action especially when accompanied by conviction of divine influence."* Okay. That sounds amazing "An inner impulse." I like that. But I don't want just ANY pulse. I want GOD'S pulse in my heart. How to I find that?

A conversation with my Pastor pointed me further down this path. When I asked him directly "How do I find my calling?" he asked me two simple yet profound questions.

"What would you do every day all day... for free?

And Why?"

He also said, "If you want to know what you're called to do, look back to see what you've been trained to do."

I went home that day with a lot to think about. After a time of soul searching, I decided to write my resume beginning in high school. I listed jobs, voluntary and paid, community involvement, clubs, and anything else I could think of.

After I wrote my resume, I went back and noted what I loved about working in those jobs in the margins. A pattern began to emerge. I realized that PEOPLE were a constant.

From helping my brother in high school at the local car wash where customers would let me wash their cars for extra money, to the retail sales jobs I had in college. I had a passion for people, for sales, and for helping get people to the things they were looking for. Whether it be a product or a service, helping and serving people were part of my purpose for sure.

Next, as I continued to study the patterns, I realized that there were many 'cheerleading' roles. I remembered the retail job in college where I was promoted into an assistant manager's position. What I loved about that position was that my main responsibilities were to organize, train, and encourage (cheerlead) the salespeople under me to be better in their positions. I would create incentive contest, teach them about product lines, train them about how to sense a customer's needs before they realize they needed it, and encourage them to be the number one salesperson in the store.

Eventually, when the manager of my store moved to bigger and better things, I was offered the position of manager. I reluctantly accepted the challenge because I was not sure I was the best person for the task. But as a young married couple living on a police officer's salary, the pay raise was impossible to pass up.

I ended up hating every single day I was in the manager's role.

Every. Single. Day.

As the senior manager of the store my days were filled with financial reports, profit and loss statements, company rankings, theft reports, cash drawer losses, hiring and firing, and dealing with disgruntled employees and customers. For years after I left that job, I believed I had failed at being a manager. I thought that the experience (and the fact that I did not enjoy it) meant that I was not qualified to be in a position of leadership and that I had forfeited any future opportunity to be successful in a position of high authority or leadership.

It took me years to realize that I had not failed at being a manager like I had told myself for so long. The truth was that I didn't thrive in that position because what I was called to do was no longer part of my role. The encouraging, organizing, and cheerleading that my assistant manager's position required (the part of the job that made me excited to go to work every day) had stayed in the position of Assistant Manager as I moved to the role of manager. The role of the manager was NOT my purpose but cheerleading, organizing, training, and supporting my manager and team were!

For months, I continued to study my resume. As more patterns emerged, I checked in with my Pastor and explained what I had learned. He confirmed from his leadership position in my life what I had discovered, and he helped me put it into a 'missions statement' of sorts.

My Mission Statement: AKA Purpose

> *I am a cheerleader, encourager, and teacher. I am a GREAT Assistant Manager and thrive in supporting others in their roles. I enjoy training others and I am a (borderline psychotic) organized person. I love affecting the lives of people all over the world to change THEIR personal worlds. And I specifically love building up other women. If those women happen to own a business, I am their biggest cheerleader!*

I know. It's a little wordy, but let's face it...so am I.

When you are not sure what to do when an opportunity comes up, take some advice from my grandmother, Lillian Payne. Be FAT.

- Faithful
- Available
- Teachable

Be Faithful: to the Lord first and foremost. When you are faithful to something, you are committed, dedicated, and loyal to it. Be trustworthy and reliable. Be faithful with the job you have and the opportunities it gives you. Be on time, be kind to your fellow teammates, be dependable.

Be Available: Be ready to try something new if God ask it of you (like writing a book!). Do not automatically decline an opportunity just because it doesn't look like your perfect picture of God's plan for your life. Jeremiah 29:11 says, *"I know the plans that **I** have for your life..."* (which means that though they are not YOUR plans) "they are good plans, to give you a future and a hope." Be prayerfully available for your next chapter and listen for the Holy Spirit (that still, small voice) to lead you to and through the doors that are part of His plan.

Be Teachable: Do you know the total number of galaxies in the universe? No?

Then realize that you do not know everything which means you have an opportunity to learn something. Your teacher may be someone older than you...or even younger than you! Do not be hard hearted. Be willing to be taught. Strive to listen more than you speak.

If you will get FAT and remain that way, you will position yourself to be used by God in new and adventurous ways. As we walk through doors of opportunity, God will help us to understand if we are on the right path. Our part in His plan is that we prayerfully continue to walk through the doors that He opens for us. Take the job opportunities that you feel the Lord is giving you. Stretch yourself a little. Be brave.

When I accepted the position of store manager in that retail store, it was a wonderful opportunity and it stretched me. It blessed my husband and I financially and I learned so many things about leadership. So many people around me believed that I would make the best store manager because of all that I had accomplished as an assistant manager. I knew on the first day that it was not for me. Did I make a wrong decision? I do not believe so. I learned something I did not know about myself. I now knew that I did not want or need to be the person in charge. I wanted to be the one that SUPPORTED the person in charge.

A Calling is a strange creature to nail down.

While driving back home to Beaumont from my parents' house in Cleveland, Texas I was discussing all of this with my daughter when she very wisely stated "but mom, my resume is so short. I don't have any patterns." She has been in college since high school and had been a Waitr driver for extra money. It is true. She has not been on the planet as long as I had but that didn't mean there were not patterns. She had patterns of creativity, inquisitiveness, and spontaneity. I explained that you don't have to have a resume for God to call you. Your LIFE is your resume. Then it dawned on me.

Callings must be developed.

I used the example of a polaroid camera photo. We all love when it pops out of the camera, but you must wait for it to develop over time. Impatient red heads like myself would wave it in the air trying to get it to reveal its secret sooner and if you blew on it and accidently spit on it, it would leave a permanent mark. As I drove, I continued to explain to her that it takes time to develop a calling. She was still being trained.

It was about that time that I glanced over to see a confusing look on my daughter's face. My sweet 22-year-old said "Mom, what are you talking about?" She had NO IDEA what a Polaroid camera was. The rest of the drive consisted of googling "polaroid" and watching videos of how they worked. Oh well. Hopefully. she got it.

Psalms 119:105 says it best, "*Your word is a lamp for my feet, a light on my path.*" In today's translation that would mean His Word is like headlights for the near future and a spotlight for the long-term. His Word will give you what you need to function safely today and still give you vision for your future. Give it time. Better yet, give it God's time. Let it develop on His pace. You might spit on it and mess it up.

~Homework~

Answer these questions:

Take your time.

Take a week…or a month.

Really ponder the answers to these questions.

1. What brings you joy? What would you do for FREE?

____

____

____

____

____

2. What makes you excited?

____

____

____

____

____

3. What makes you feel fulfilled?

____

____

____

____

____

List three things that you have enjoyed doing in your life and what you loved most about them. Include volunteer positions, non-paid and church leadership positions.

a. ____

____

____

____

Positives:

____

____

____

b. ____

____

____

____

Positives:

____

____

____

c. ____

____

____

____

Positives:

____

____

____

After spending some time meditating on the previous questions, formulate a mission/calling statement of your own. Be as wordy as you would like!

Chapter 4

Finding My Assignment

Assignments are meant to be temporary focused mini missions accomplished for God. Once an assignment is completed, we are to move on to our next assignment. If we are not careful, we will get our job and our assignments confused.

In my case, I thought my job was my identity. Because I was confused, I was failing my assignment. I had completely missed the assignment handout and was busy doing what I thought the teacher should have wanted from me. I never heard the teacher explain the real goal He wanted me to accomplish. I was too caught up in what I wanted the assignment to be.

My job made me feel as if I had a place to go, people who needed me, and goals to accomplish. My paycheck felt like a reward for my service and an occasional "atta-girl" made me feel appreciated. All good things, but because I had missed the assignment and turned in something completely different, I had failed the assignment. I had done a good work, but it wasn't the work God had asked me to do. I had my Identity and my assignment mixed up.

There are several scenarios you may find yourself in right now. Maybe you love your job or chapter of life, maybe you don't. Or maybe you are feeling indifferent, not inspired but not tortured either. If you are feeling as though you have lost or have begun to lose your identity in your job or chapter of life let me help you get your focus back.

But I love my job!

When we love our jobs, it is easy to get our identity, calling, and assignment mixed up. We like showing up, we feel accomplished and useful. If that is you, (and it was me too!) I am happy for you. But I challenge you to be careful not to lose your identity in your job. Because, if you suddenly lose our wonderful job, your identity is crushed, and you can feel like you have lost calling or purpose (ask me how I know!)

I recently watched an interview with a man who had lost his job due to the Covid-19 Pandemic.

Interviewer: "Is Disney (his job) part of your identity?

Gentleman: "It's not part of my identity. It IS my identity."

Clearly, he loved his job. After all, Disney is supposed to be the happiest place on earth. He had completely emersed himself in his work. Everything that made him feel useful, needed, appreciated and worthy was tied up in his position. Now that he had lost it, he was devastated. What he didn't realize was he had worked for one of the most successful companies in the world, and it had prepared him for future opportunity. He just could not see them. His assignment had changed locations, but his calling had been honed during his time at Disney.

The interview ended with a somber picture of tears running down his face. He had lost his identity in his job and now was confused as to what to do next. He needed to firmly establish his identity and calling then single out where his next assignment was located and focus on that.

Jobs come and go. We can get laid off. We may even get fired (been there, done that!). If you lose your job move on. Get another one. Do not get stuck in that muddy pit of despair that your entire world is tied up in that job. Do not be bitter and spiteful. Realize that your assignment location is changing. Ask God to show you how and where to go next. Find your next paycheck and assignment but realize they may or may not be in the same place!

What if my job is not a happy place for me and I don't see my assignment?

For some of us, our jobs DON'T feel like the happiest place on earth. They are a weight that grips our neck every Monday morning. Perhaps you work in a place that is sometimes hostile or your boss does not appreciate you. You may feel stuck or even trapped. If you're not careful, you can begin to allow the toxicity and lack of fulfillment to define your identity in a negative or even hurtful way. It will begin to change the way you think about yourself and others. It can harden your heart and warp your perspective of the world, sinners, and even Jesus Christ.

If you've gotten this far and realized through some soul searching that your current job is not your calling but just a paycheck, then you may be thinking... time to quit. But hold your horses' partner. That's not what I'm talking about here.

Yes, I certainly wish your job were something that you enjoyed, but this homework is not about quitting your current bill-paying position but looking at your JOB and YOUR ASSIGNMENT as two different things that MAY be in the same spot.

The Bible has several examples of people who had tough jobs but still had assignments that they needed to pass to move on to the greater things God had for them.

Genesis 37 begins telling a story of a man named Joseph who had a job that was hostile to say the least. He had been sold into slavery by his older brothers to some Midianite traders and later sold in Egypt to a man named Potiphar. Joseph had been forced into labor at a job he didn't want and hadn't sought out. But the Bible says that *"The Lord was with Joseph, so he succeeded in everything he did as he served in the home of his Egyptian master."* (Genesis 39:2). Even though it wasn't his dream job, I believe he recognized that he had an assignment while he was there. While he served his current 'master,' he continued to please God. He was FAT!

Be faithful to show up like Joseph did, maintain an attitude that is becoming of a child of God and be the best employee you can be. In the meantime, seek the Word of God, pray for guidance, and listen to what He may need you to do while you are there. Sometimes, it's not what you're going through but what you're going to!

Later, Joseph was wrongfully accused of an unlawful act against a member of Potiphar's family and was thrown into prison. Yet, even there, he looked for an assignment. His situation had changed (in fact, it got worse!) but it didn't change the fact that he had an assignment.

If Joseph were not careful, he could have easily slipped into a place of bitterness and anger. Instead, he looked for the assignments in each situation and passed them to the best of his abilities. God did the rest. (Go read the full story in Genesis chapters 37-47. Best. Ending. Ever!)

My pastor, Ron Hammonds says it this way, "Be EXTRA in your ordinary!"

What if my job is just a job!

Maybe your job isn't terrible but it's not your calling either. It's neutral. A necessity to pay the bills. The people are not horrible, but you feel indifferent about the job you were hired to do. It doesn't give you immense joy, but you don't hate it either. Maybe you're someone who is not career oriented, but a job is a necessity of adulting. I get it.

Philippians 2:14-15 gives you some direction.

> *"Do everything without complaining and arguing, so that no one can criticize you. Live clean, innocent lives as children of God, shining like bright lights in a world full of crooked and perverse people." (New Living Translation)*

I love this quote by Marin Luther King Jr. ***"… (a street sweeper) should sweep streets even as Michelangelo painted, or Beethoven composed music or Shakespeare wrote poetry. He should sweep streets so well that all the hosts of heaven and earth will pause to say, 'Here lived a great street sweeper who did his job well."***

Colossians 3:17 says *"And whatever you do, whether in word or deed, do it all in the name of the Lord Jesus, giving thanks to God the Father through him."*

Work your job faithfully to the glory of God. It may be that WHILE working in that job, you may also work your assignment. Perhaps the reason you are at THAT job is to fulfill a current assignment. If you're struggling with not enjoying your current job, ask the Lord to show you an assignment while you're there. Perhaps a co-worker, client or customer needs the light of Christ in their life and you're it. Or someone around you needs encouragement or needs to watch as you walk through a challenging time in your life so that when they are faced with the same challenge, they run to you to ask how you made it through. What an opportunity to be bright light!

One of my favorite stories is in Acts 16:25-26, when Paul and Silas are in prison. Around midnight they were praying and singing hymns to God and the Bible says that, '*the other prisoners were listening.*' When you are going through life, other "prisoners" (people just like you, caught in tough situations, feeling trapped) are watching to see how YOU (perhaps the only believer in Jesus they know!) handles it.

Fulfilling your assignment may determine how long you stay there. Remember, it's not what you're going THROUGH but what you're going TO, that matters most. (Pastor Ron Hammonds, Point to Ponder #179). For Paul and Silas, what they were going THROUGH was terrible. They were unjustly imprisoned and had been severely beaten (verse 23), but HOW they went through it made a difference to the people that were also stuck in the same prison as they were (including one guy that worked there). Their physical AND spiritual chains were broken off because Paul and Silas were not afraid to accept a tough assignment. But here is the reality, their physical situation had not changed. They were still in prison. Other people need to see the Jesus in you while in this prison we sometimes call life.

What if my job is not my current assignment?

A job is, by definition, a place where you go to receive financial payment for performing a service or a task that may or may not be repeated daily.

A calling, however, is what God created you to do. How you worship Him, serve Him, and honor Him while using your talents (God given and irrevocable) and strengths to glorify God on planet Earth. How can you take the mission/calling statement that you wrote in section 2 of this workbook and apply it elsewhere in your life?

I know several worship leaders who are clearly called to be 'lead worshippers,' but who are forced to hold down the traditional 8-5 job outside of their church roles. Does that make them less called? Absolutely not. Their calling is to lead worship. Their current assignment is to do it anywhere.

An assignment can be not only fulfilled but exemplified and even amplified to a hurting world by going to your current "job." The lead worshippers I know lead others to worship no matter where they are, and in more ways than just singing while they work. They are examples of how to worship God in the ordinary parts of our everyday lives. They are being EXTRA in their ordinary.

Americans spend an average of 34.4 hours a week at their jobs but there are 168 hours in a week. That is 133.6 hours in your week that you are not earning a paycheck. That's a lot of time. It's true. A job can just be a job. It is very possible that your biggest assignment is NOT at your job. If your job is not your current assignment, ask God to show you where your assignment is? Assignments are job but jobs are not necessarily your assignment.

What if I don't have a job?

If you need to get a job, and are physically able, do so. And my pastor would say that you have a forty hour a week job finding a job until you do. But not having a job does not mean you don't have an assignment. You have an assignment even if you don't have a job. Maybe it's to wash windows at your church or help an elderly neighbor with their yard. No job does not get you off the hook from finding and working your current assignment.

To all my retired friends out there, you're not off the hook either. You still have an assignment. Where can you volunteer, train, or pour into the lives of others? Maybe your chapter has changed, and the locations are different, but every day you walk and breathe on planet Earth, God has an assignment for you.

Maybe you lost your job (or chose to leave your job) to go home and be a full or part time stay-at-home parent. Congratulations, you have just landed the greatest full-time job of all time (WAY more than 34.4 hours/week). Your new position pays in dividends that may look differently than the ones you received on your last paycheck, but the rewards will be amazing. It still does not mean that you do not have an assignment. Maybe your assignment right now is to help your teenager navigate junior high drama, pass Algebra, or give your grandchildren a soft place to land in this crazy world. You are raising adults; you just happen to have them in their childhood years. Pass these assignments! 34.4 hours a week at another job or not. They are the most important assignments you have been entrusted with completing.

A job can be just a job but challenge yourself to always keep your eyes opened to what God may be asking you to do, be or say. Someone is watching you parent or grandparent. They are watching how you react to the changes, pressures and challenges in life, and you will be a light to them.

So, whether you have job or don't, love it or just tolerate it, your heavenly father ALWAYS has a job for you to do. You have an assignment that needs to be accepted and accomplished. When you try your best to find and ace these assignments, it prepares you for the next bigger, better, and perhaps even more difficult assignments. If you don't complete the assignment, you are in right now, you may struggle when the next challenges arise.

Pass the test.

What if I don't like the assignment He gives me?

It is entirely possible that your assignments might not be easy, fun, or exciting. I'm sure Joseph didn't exactly swoon when he realized his current assignment was to serve as a slave in a foreign land. God may ask you to do something that pushes you out of your comfort zone (like writing a book!). He may ask you to leave something behind or pick something up. You may be asked to love someone who is unlovable or ungrateful.

Accept the challenge!

Muscles are only made stronger when you work and stretch them. The workout may even hurt a little but you're building your strength each time you pick up those weights. Each workout (assignment) works specific muscles that God needs you to strengthen for future assignments.

Think of it this way, when you were in school aren't you grateful that the teacher taught addition BEFORE she taught Algebra? Algebra is hard enough but to ask someone to pass that test without the proper training would be unfair. Yet how many of us were not paying enough attention in the earlier assignments so that when the tough ones were handed out, we were ill prepared and underqualified to accept the challenge much less pass the test.

Show up. Do the work. Your next chapter depends on it.

Yes, you will make mistakes, but God is not looking for perfection.

He is looking for obedience.

That being said, you do have a choice here. You could opt in or opt out of these assignments. Rebekah, in the book of Genesis (Chapter 24) opted IN when the servant of Abraham asked if she wanted to go back with him to a foreign land and marry a complete stranger (NOT A PROPHETIC WORD FOR YOU TODAY!). She could have said no. In a rare Biblical moment, her family actually asked her if she wanted to marry Isaac. She said yes! And by doing so found herself in the family line of Jesus.

Chapter 5

The Continuation

I know what you're asking. WAIT! How do I find my assignment?!?

That is a conversation between you and God. Only God hands out assignments.

I wish there was a workbook page with a quick answer for me to give you in a fancy and easy to remember one-liner, but there is not. The only way to get your assignment is to spend time with God.

As I said in the 'How to read this book' section of the Introduction chapter, this journey took me four and a half years to walk. This book is meant to be a roadmap to point you in the right direction. My hope is that by the time you had reached this sentence you had worked the first two sections of the book. In doing that, you would have spent some serious time with God. This takes time and it takes tuning your ears to hear what the voice of God is speaking to you. Tuning your ears happens when you spend time in prayer and in the Word of God. It is a relationship.

When I was in high school, I played basketball. My father was not always able to come to my games because he worked a significant distance from our school. But somehow, when he was able to show up, over the sounds of the gym, I could hear his voice. Even if I didn't know he was going to be there, I would hear his voice through the chaos.

I am a daddy's girl and I had tuned my ears to the sound of his voice. He did not have to yell, in fact, he never did. His voice has always been steady and calm. That is how our Heavenly father speaks, but you must tune your ears. And the only way to do that is through spending time with him. When you tune your ears, even the storms cannot silence the voice of the Lord.

Roadmap to finding your assignment:

1. Be sure your identity is founded in Christ alone by studying His Word. This step must be repeated daily to remind ourselves. We can so easily forget.
2. Look back on what you've been trained to do to narrow down your calling and realize that your calling is always developing.
3. Then wait for God to reveal your current assignment. You must be emersed in His Word and listening for His still small voice. He will tell you. Continue to listen and ask until He answers.

Matthew 7:7 says, *"Ask and it will be given to you; seek and you will find; knock and the door will be opened to you."*

I was ready for a new assignment.

I was NOT ready for what He handed me.

After months of waiting, praying, and I will admit, even begging. He opened my ears again one morning with a quiet subtle voice and my new assignment... "study the Word and serve your husband."

That's not quite what I was expecting.

But I know that it is what I am currently assigned to do and so, knowing that my calling is to encourage, support, and resource, I began looking for ways to do that for Darren and started carving out time to study the Word more consistently.

When I began to really mediate on the assignment, I realized that the word 'serve' to many people has a negative connotation. It is sometimes translated to being a slave or a doormat. But Mark 10:45 talks about Jesus serving when it says, *"even the Son of Man did not come to be served but to serve, and to give his life as a ransom for many."* Thank goodness, God was only asking me to serve ONE man, not all of them. And he is an exceptionally good man.

I began to ask God HOW to serve Darren and he has shown me specific and general ways to do so. I certainly try to serve him by keeping a somewhat clean home, cooking dinner, and doing his laundry. In a very specific way, the Lord encouraged me to make sure that his recliner was ready for him, and the living room was clean (with the remotes to the television easily accessible by his chair) so that when he came home from working so hard, he could kick off his boots and relax. The more I ask the Lord the more specifically He gives me little practical ways to bless him. To serve him.

He recently showed me that I've been asked to not only serve him dinner but also serve him some patience when he needs it, some kindness when he is grumpy or not feeling well, and some encouragement when he is feeling overwhelmed. And although I have failed at this many times, and these tend to be harder to serve sometimes than dinner, I am trying my best knowing that God is cultivating a strength in me that I will need for future assignments.

As well, I am serving my husband by helping him in the various business ventures he has and doing everything from running errands and helping him at some of our investments properties to cutting up dead deer (one of his companies is a deer processing company in Port Neches, Texas) to the glory of God. I am far from perfect, but God knows I am trying my best.

I am also blessed to be a part of the most amazing Bible study at my church where I get to be the biggest cheerleader to women in our church and share the Word of God and how it has changed my life in so many ways. This has helped me to devote more consistent time to the study of God's Word.

Chapter 6

The Conclusion

If you lose your identity, you may miss your calling and fail your assignment!

Read that again.

If you lose your identity by placing it in something other than Jesus Christ (job, money, spouse, kids, ministry, etc.), you may miss your highest calling (those gifts that are irrevocable) and fail the current assignment God has for you!

The story of the Rich Young Ruler in Luke 18 is an example of someone who because his identity was in the wrong thing, failed to accept a tough but rewarding assignment. The story goes like this...

Jesus was walking from the Galilee toward Jerusalem when the rich young ruler came running up to him, knelt and asked Jesus *"What must I do to inherit eternal life?"*

Jesus answered him by saying *"...you know the commandants: You must not murder. You must not commit adultery. You must not steal. You must not testify falsely. You must not cheat anyone. Honor your mother and father."* The man replied that he had kept those laws since he was young.

Then Jesus looked at him with genuine love and said, *"There is still one thing you haven't done, Go and sell all your possessions and give to the poor, and you will have treasure in Heaven. Then come, follow me." At this, the man's face fell, and he went away sad, for he had many possessions.* (Matthew 19:16-30, Mark 10:17-31 and Luke 18:18-30)

That is a tough assignment. And I will admit, I probably would have failed this one too. I don't think I'm strong enough to sell all I have and give it away. But this story reminds me that we can easily lose our identities in the things we have. In his case, his identity was tied up in his wealth and the role it afforded him.

Jesus was clearly looking for someone with great wealth to give to the poor for some reason. Just one chapter later in the Luke version of this story, Jesus finds another rich man (who happens to be an unbeliever at the time) who IS willing to accept an assignment. Zacchaeus gave HALF of his wealth to the poor and to those he had cheated (he was a tax collector) he gave back four times as much.

The rich young ruler didn't realize that what he had been perfectly positioned for the greatest and toughest assignment of his life. The reward is at the end of verse 22. "You will have treasures in Heaven. Then come, follow me." A permanent reward in Heaven waiting for him, and an earthly reward of walking with Christ. But again, I probably would not have been able to do it either.

I've thought of this young man many times, wondering if he had missed previous assignments that would have made this decision easier. Wondering if he regretted the decision, he made that day later in his life? Did he tell his grandchildren not make the same decision? Maybe, when he heard that Jesus had been crucified, he realized his error and then sold all his possessions to give to the poor. I hope so.

For years, I misplaced my identity and it cost me precious time in walking in the calling and assignments that the Lord had for me. My prayer for you is that you firmly establish your identity in Christ and remind yourself often (even daily) of where it should be. It can so easily slip away if we are not vigilant. I pray that you continue to hone your calling and gifts as you walk out your relationship with Christ, allowing him to point you in different arenas of life that you may not have imagined you would find yourself stepping into.

And lastly, I pray that you can easily identify the next assignment as the chapters in your life transition and change. May you ever be drawn to your next assignment, eager to see what God has laid out for you to do as part of His great plan.

May you never forget that you are a child of the King. He created you to do a specific work for him and it is one that He needs you to do for His glory. Do not ever think that you are anything less than chosen, called, and equipped to do what He has prepared you to do. He is building a future for you and building you for that future.

Don't let the world convince you that you need to be 'more' of something or 'less' of something. To be more quiet or less quiet. To be more successful or less successful. You are a masterpiece created in the heart of our Father God.

You are nothing less than the exact picture that God designed you to be. Your talents and callings are irreversible, you cannot deny them or give them back. You were created for such a time as this and if you will walk in the identity, calling and assignment that God has placed on your life, you will be an amazing light in this murky world. You are a treasure.

~Scriptures about your Identity in Christ~

Grab a spiral notebook and in your own handwriting copy these scriptures then write how they apply to your life and your identity.

What thoughts about your identity do you need to change?

Ephesians 2:5
Ephesians 2:10
1 Corinthians 12:27
1 Peter 2:9
Deuteronomy 14:2
Jeremiah 1:5
Romans 5:7-9
1 John 1:9
1 John 3:1
2 Corinthians 1:22
Romans 6:18
Isaiah 43:4
1 John 4:19
Genesis 1:27
Zephaniah 3:17
Philippians 2:5
Philippians 4:7
1 John 4:4
Psalms 139:14
1 Corinthians 6:20
Proverbs 31:10
Romans 8:17
2 Corinthians 5:20
1 Corinthians 5:20
1 Corinthians 6:19
John 15:15
1 Peter 2:24
2 Timothy 1:7
James 4:7
Psalms 94:14
Isaiah 66:1-2

Citations:

Brad Lomenick; Mark Burnett, (2015). *H3 Leadership – Be Hungry, Stay Humble, Always Hustle.* Nashville, Tennessee: Nelson Books, an imprint of Thomas Nelson, [2015] ©2015

"Calling." Merriam-Webster.com Dictionary, Merriam-Webster, https://www.merriam-webster.com/dictionary/calling. Accessed 16 Jul. 2021.

Holy Bible, New Living Translation, 1996/2015

SOAP EXAMPLES

O - "a man of standing" -
- wealthy *similar to David "mighty men of valor"
- had integrity
- good business man
- recognized at the gate of the city
- able to facilitate needs.
- willing to facilitate / meet needs
- Leader

A GOOD MAN!

A - We should all pray that God makes our men "men of standing" (or pray for future husbands)

P - "God, thank you that I married a Boaz

VS 2 - "

S "And Ruth, the Moabitess said to Naomi, "Let me go to the fields and pick up the leftover grain behind anyone whose eyes I find favor"

RUTH: "I'M BORED!"

O - Ruth is referred to as 'the Moabitess'. Again, this is to clarify that she was a foreigner / and an alien in this land she was in

(So are we!)

"Grace" def: favor when it's undeserved"

S-VS3 - "So she went out and began to glean in the fields behind the harvesters. As it turns out, she found herself working in the (a) fields belonging to Boaz, who was from the clan of Elimelech. — LOOKING FOR GRACE

O- "As it turns out" - ☺

A - Amazing how God puts us right where we need to be even when we don't realize it. — Psalms 23

P- God, help me remember that we have all the while been in your field. You are ready, willing and able to take care of us. Help me to trust you... even in my unbelief.

S- vs 4 "Just then Boaz arrived from Bethlehem and greeted the harvesters, "The Lord be with you!"

O- How good is it to know that God has good people living in bad times!

- Have you ever felt like you're the only one going through this and every one is against you? (1 Kings 19:18) There were 7000 more!

God's never late he's always on time!

S-V9 – "Watch the field where the men are harvesting, and follow along after the girls. I have told the men not to ~~tho~~ touch you. And when you are thirsty, go and drink from the water jars * the men have filled."

O – first sexual harassment policy ☺

– Boaz is protecting her by

A. Telling the workers not to touch her

B. Telling her to stay in his fields.

– She had found "favor" from Boaz

Favor = approval, support, or liking for someone or something

– An act of kindness beyond what is due or usual.

Theme: Christ showed us favor undeserved, unusual and beyond

A – God has showed us undeserved favor and protection because He loved us (Before we loved Him). He noticed us before we knew He existed. He FIRST loved us!

P – Thank you Jesus! For all the love and favor undeserved!

* She got to drink water drawn for her!

* extraordinary concern for her provision + protection.

Acknowledgements

As I began thinking of writing these acknowledgements, I realized that the people I wanted to thank came in two categories. My inspiration and my motivation.

So here goes…

My Inspiration:

First, my amazing husband, Darren Creel.

For the last 28 years, he has supported everything I have ever wanted to try. Except for skydiving! He was not okay with me trying that, and although he said I could do it if I *really* felt I needed to, I knew he was uncomfortable with the risk, so I passed. At least for now.

But even then, He has been an amazing support. This kind of safety net, friendship and encouragement bolsters me to try anything. From studying for my appraiser's license and investing in peer-to-peer lending for women in Africa, to writing this book, he has always been a voice of reason, but never said no. And he has always paid for the venture with our hard-earned money. The most amazing part is that when my ideas go south and flop hard (and a few have!), he has NEVER made me feel guilty. That kind of foundation makes a girl feel like she can do anything.

I remember when I told him that I felt I needed to publish this book. I had done all the research. I knew the metrics and the risk. I knew the financial and time commitments it would take to get it to the finish line. I presented the idea to him, and his response was perfect. "It's going to be cool to say that I have an author as a wife." Thank you Handsome. You are the best.

My baby girl, Kate Lynn Creel.

Kate is our only child and, honestly, she is a miracle. She was born extremely premature, three months early weighing only 4lbs and 12 ounces. She spent eighteen days in the Neonatal Intensive Care Unit at St. Elizabeth's hospital in Beaumont, Texas where she won the hearts of every doctor and nurse who came in contact with her. She has been a fighter since day one. She is also an artist, the best travel buddy (we have been all over the world), and the most loyal friend anyone could ever have. She is 100% red head, but she loves Jesus, her Momma and Daddy, and her puppy, Grumpy boy.

It was the letter that I wrote to her that inspired this book. She is now 24 years old and working on her second degree at Lamar Institute of Technology in our hometown of Beaumont, Texas. She just recently put an offer in on her second and third investment property (she bought her first one at the tender age of 21 and remodeled it almost completely by herself). Daddy and I enormously proud of you Katie-bug. You have inspired me to do many things, and it is one of your greatest callings…to inspire.

My Mom and Dad, Royce and Jennifer Cooper

You know those TV shows when you were growing up where the mom had snacks on the table when you got home from school and wore an apron? That was not my mom!

And I am so glad!

My mom, Jennifer Cooper, was the mom that was working tirelessly to forge the way for every student at her school to be able to pursue the dream they wanted. She worked countless hours inspiring kids and their parents to find a way to make dreams happen. She was the principal of a private Christian school in Cleveland, Texas called Heritage Christian Academy, and countless adults can now look back on their years as a student there and give her a great deal of credit for being tough in the most caring and compassionate way.

She too is an author and has bolstered many teachers and administrators to continue the incredibly difficult, many times thankless, but always rewarding work of raising the next generation through education.

When I told her that I wanted to do this she said, "Do it!" Thanks, Mom. You have inspired me in every single arena and chapter of my life. I will never be able to repay you or sufficiently vocalize your impact. Never.

My father, Royce Cooper, is a quiet man and worked for the State of Texas as we were growing up, but every Saturday you would find him in the yard, in the barn or in the garden. In fact, my earliest memory is carrying a big ol' glass of Momma's sweet tea across the yard to him in the summer heat. I vividly remember trying not to spill it.

He is also a wood-working genius and has a tool for everything. And I mean EVERYTHING. If you walk through a flea market with Dad, he will find a tool he needs. Many times, Darren and I have called on him to help us with the original front door on a property that needed a miracle to survive, or a special tool to dismantle something that had seized up. He has created and built by hand, a special gift for each of his grandchildren's sixteenth birthdays, built yard games for my nieces' wedding, and countless other projects that have blessed so many.

Until he recently stepped off the Deacon board at his home church in Cleveland, TX, he had been a deacon since he was sixteen years old (as a Junior Deacon then continuously ever since). That speaks volumes to the kind of integrity and character this man has. He has been walking with Jesus for the entirety of his life and it is evident to everyone around him. When Royce Cooper speaks, even softly, people listen because they know he hears from God.

Dad was the one that became the most emphatic about me writing a book. In recent years, I had begun to write online journal entries and occasionally share them on social media to, hopefully, encourage others. He shared one called "Dry Bones" with his siblings during a reunion. I have yet to expand that one into the book he thinks it should be, but I do have a desire to please my Daddy so do not be surprised.

I had posted the letter to Kate that was the original inspiration for this book on social media for just a few hours for a friend to download in the middle of 2020. Just a week or so later, Dad was rushed to the hospital with severe abdominal pains. I spent the next several days sitting in my truck in the hospital parking lot while Mom sat with Dad in the hospital. The first night, Mom and I drove back to their house in Cleveland to rest. When I sat down in Dad's recliner, to my right on a side table, was the letter. In the few hours it was there, he had downloaded and printed it and had been reading it in his chair.

The next day, I bought lunch for Mom, and while she sat in my truck to eat it, I went up to sit with Dad. In his hospital room I asked him about it. He again encouraged me (and again, emphatically) that I needed to write a book.

So Daddy, here we are. I cannot thank you enough for seeing things in me that I could not see in myself and for encouraging me to go after them. From basketball scholarships to standard shift trucks, you have always thought I could do more than I thought I could and because of that… I have.

My motivation:

Until June 24th, 2021, just a little more than a month or so before the official launch date of this book, only about a dozen or so people knew the book even existed. As I expanded the original letter into the current format, I became almost paralyzed with the fear that either God would NEVER be able to use or that He WOULD.

Because of the paralysis, I had not shared with very many people even the idea of writing the book. But there were a few, and they have been my motivation to get it out there. Without these amazing people…it would have never happened.

Dawn Fulkerson Guevara.

My friend Dawn Guevara is the director of an amazing ministry called Purity Revelation (www.purityrevelation.org) in Phoenix, Arizona. The ministry has an arm called Lotus Loft that provides housing and meets needs of mothers and their children in homeless situations. She and all that her family accomplishes through this ministry are amazing.

After Dad's hospital stay and the conversation about writing this book, I had a long drive home to ponder the idea. When I told the Lord, I was not even sure where to START, God brought Dawn to my mind. Dawn's mother, Mrs. Sandy Fulkerson, is the bestselling author of *Bread Crumbs on Purpose*, and *Harvest: The Field of Hope* (both available on Amazon!). On October 18, 2020, I messaged Dawn and asked her which publisher Mrs. Sandy used for her publishing. It was her email to the publisher and her pointing me in the right direction that put my foot on the actual path to getting this done.

As I drafted the book, the ladies that Dawn work with were a continuous motivation to me. If I could get this roadmap into the hands of women who needed a practical yet simple plan to follow, and if it made a difference then I would deem this project a success.

Thank you Dawn. For all that you do for women and mothers everywhere, but especially for supporting me with this venture.

Pastor Ron Hammonds

I do not quite know how to put into words how to thank this man. He is an inspiration and motivation to so many and he has been my pastor since before Darren and I married. In fact, I met him the week that I met Darren.

Darren had just returned from deployment in Desert Storm the day I met him at the Nederland Texas Recreational Center. His high school friend, Tom Riley introduced us. The next weekend, Darren asked me to join him at church, where Pastor Ron was now the Senior Pastor. Darren had just met him earlier that week as well.

I will never forget walking into the church when Pastor Ron met us on the sidewalk just outside the front doors. He introduced himself to me and eventually asked what I was studying at Lamar University. I was a Deaf Education Major at Lamar, which meant I was fluent in American Sign Language. Darren and I visited with him for a moment and proceeded to sit on the back left hand side of the church, about five or six rows from the back and just a few seats off the side aisle.

Just as church was starting, Darren ran to the restroom leaving me sitting safely in my comfy blue chair. Now, I did not know of course (and neither did Darren at the time) that Pastor Ron had a thing called 'Mix, Meet, Mingle and Multiply!,' a moment, just after we stand to sing the first song when the church members greet each other, meet new people, and hug some necks. Darren had "conveniently" disappeared (if you know Darren you know he is not a hugger) and there I was, a new girl who had fallen in love with this Army boy and was at a new church sitting all alone. I must have had a deer-in-headlights look on my face when I looked up on the stage at Pastor Ron because he looked straight at me and signed three simple signs.

OK.
Fine.
Sit down.

Those signs translated in my head to "It's okay, it'll be fine. Just have a seat."

From that moment, I knew this was my new church.

Pastor Ron is quoted in this book many times, because through the year it has been the life principals that we have gleaned from him that have helped us to grow in our marriage, raise our little family, and build our businesses. We call them "Ron-isms;" he calls them Points to Ponder.

Pastor Ron, I am certain these Points to Ponder are embedded in this book in places I cannot even see. They have been so deeply planted in our everyday lives that we just live these principals without being able to reference back to a specific sermon or conversation. And I know you prefer to reap your applause on the other side of Heaven but my biggest fear in writing this book is that I did not give you credit for something you said that so dramatically shifted my life toward Jesus and helped me become more like Him.

Thank you.

Thank you for believing in our little family. Thank you for taking me all over the world and showing me how to be the hands and feet of Jesus. Thank you for the countless conversations. But most importantly thank you (and Brenda) for living a life of selfless sacrifice, consistent faith, and complete authenticity in front of us. We are so much better for it.

Just for the record, our favorite Point to Ponder is "Make a living, Make a Life, Make a Difference." It has been our family motto since Kate was young.

Robin McEachen

Robin is a wife, mom, vital member of our volunteer church leadership, English teacher in our local public school system and a key part of our Ladies Bible Study called Bible 101. She is a well-educated, fiery, and outspoken woman of God and she is, my friend.

Robin McEachen is also the editor of this project which is a story in and of itself.

One night after bible study, she was among four women that I shared this project with as I asked them to please cover it and me in prayer. Later, Robin made herself available to me if I needed any assistance with the editing. The problem was that I had kept this project incredibly quiet and VERY few people even knew about it (at this point, I had told less than five people outside of my family).

When I got to the point that my publisher, Becky Norwood, wanted me to start interviewing editors I remembered Robin's offer but hesitated because I still was not sure I wanted anyone so geographically close to me to see me this vulnerable. I had hoped that I could put this book out there secretly.

After interviewing three other editors, it was obvious none of them were going to work for me. Darren was the one that quietly encouraged me to consider Robin. I texted her one day to ask if she would be willing to interview for the position and she cheerfully agreed. She and I met at a local coffee shop. I presented her what I was calling 'a paper' and she and I spoke candidly. As she looked over what I had written, she made some amazing suggestions, laughed at my humor on page one, and told me I needed to do this, and she wanted to help. I made the hire official a few days later, but the truth was I knew immediately. The first thing she told me to do was to stop calling it a "paper."

Robin, I can honestly say that this project would not be available today in its present form if it were not for you. Thank you for encouraging me, dealing with my love of commas and when necessary, boldly reminding me of the anointing on this project from day one. Your friendship has come to mean so much to me. Much love, "Moses"

Think Tank

I am so lucky to have a huge friendship circle. I am still friends with many from high school and college but the Holy Huddle of friendships I have in my church and specifically in our ladies Bible Study are some of the most precious. These ladies were motivating me even though they had no idea this book was even in the works.

Of those ladies, four of them specifically became what I dubbed "the Think Tank":

LeeAnn Kennedy, Casey Wells, LaVon Merritt, and Robin McEachen. They were the first four ladies I talked to about the book when it was still in its infancy. I have been able to trust them with my story, my heart, and my shortcomings.

You ladies have somehow kept me motivated by contributing your thoughts and perspectives in the most amazing ways. You have been the best sounding board for me during this project and I will miss our think tank Saturdays.

About
Susan Cooper Creel

Susan Cooper Creel is a wife to a serial entrepreneur and mom to a feisty red head. She loves to travel the world to support mission organizations, women in business and children.

She is a resourceful cheerleader, teacher, and self-proclaimed bible nerd. Her life's goal is to 'affect the lives of people all over the word to change *THEIR OWN* personal worlds' through practical support and the study of God's Word.

Susan lives in Beaumont, Texas with her husband of 28 years, Darren, and her 24-year-old daughter Kate, for whom she wrote the original letter that became this book.

We invite you to leave a review for this book,
on Amazon or Goodreads!
www.susancreel.com
https://www.facebook.com/ICA-Book-112518687763633

www.ingramcontent.com/pod-product-compliance
Lightning Source LLC
LaVergne TN
LVHW080333110826
845155LV00024B/154

* 9 7 8 1 9 5 3 8 0 6 4 8 2 *